How to Quit Chewing Tobacco for Good

Your Guide to Quit Dipping

by Donald Fosio

Table of Contents

Introduction

Quitting any habit can be hard to do, especially it's a habit that you have had for a long time. Dipping, especially, is so addictive because not only is nicotine, an addictive chemical substance involved, but also because a person gets used to the feeling of having dip in their mouth. Back to the nicotine though, did you know dipping contains even more of it than cigarettes do? That's right: a single pinch of smokeless tobacco can contain the same level of nicotine as three to four cigarettes. As a matter of fact, smokeless tobacco contains up to 3,000 chemicals that are quite harmful to the human body, dozens of which have been found to cause cancer.

Overcoming the addiction is quite possible though, as well as following through once you've quit, to make sure you don't start back up again. As with any addiction, you can expect to go through withdrawals. Of course none of this is going to be a walk in the park, but the fact that you are reading this means that you are, at the very least, thinking about quitting the habit. That's the first – and most important – step actually, so pat yourself on the back, or bump your chest with your fist, or whatever else you're into. Withdrawal symptoms you may experience include losing sleep, sores in the mouth, headaches, and anxiety. You might not experience any of these prior quitting and, for some, these withdrawal symptoms are enough to drag them back into the addiction. If you think that something does not feel right, by all means, consult a doctor; but generally speaking, these symptoms are pretty normal.

Considering that tobacco has no proven benefit to the human body, dipping is considered one of the "nastier" kinds of addiction, which is yet another reason to quit. Not to mention that tobacco can cause various types of cancers, like lung, larynx, esophagus, mouth, throat, kidney, pancreatic, bladder and stomach cancer, and even acute myeloid leukemia. And, unlike smoking cigarettes, dipping does not get rid of most of the harmful chemicals in tobacco. Second hand smoke is a lot more dangerous than smoking itself because many of the harmful chemicals, like nicotine and cyanide, are expelled through the smoke. Dipping does not give you the same convenience. Everything is absorbed by you and can cause health problems a whole lot faster than smoking.

Quitting the habit is not the easiest thing to do but, as the old saying goes, "nothing worth doing can be done overnight." The advantages of quitting are well worth all the hard work and withdrawals that you will have to endure. In this book, we will be talking about not just the *why*, but more importantly, the *how*. We will walk through understanding the addiction, knowing how to quit properly, and learning how to ultimately live a tobacco-free life. Let's get started!

Chapter 1: The Dangers of Dipping

It is a well-known fact that dipping is inherently dangerous but, being an addiction, people cannot just shake it off. The addiction has serious consequences, not just for your health, but for your social life and pocketbook too. If you have had this addiction for years, you might not have noticed, but this is true nevertheless.

Health

Dipping causes several different types of cancer, such as esophageal, mouth, pancreatic, pharynx and tongue cancer, just to name a few. Most cancer from dipping is formed in the oral cavity, since that's the part of the body that makes the most contact with the tobacco. Dipping can also increase your chances of having cavities and tooth decay. This is because tobacco, like candy, contains sugar. Also, it can disintegrate the teeth's enamel, making them weaker and more likely to experience cavities. Smokeless tobacco has also been linked to heart disease and high blood pressure, which can ultimately cause heart disease and stroke.

Financial

Other than the hospital bills that you will inevitably have to deal with later, a can of smokeless tobacco generally costs around $3-$4. If you only use two cans in a week, which is a bit conservative for most, you still end up flushing over $350+ down the drain each year, while making your health suffer. However, people who are addicted to dipping normally empty a can in a day. If you are one of those people, you are actually throwing away around $1,250 each year. Now, think of all the things that you could have bought or done with that money, instead of flushing it down the toilet (along with your health) because of your addiction.

Social

Unless you are a cowboy who only interacts with horses and cows all day, most of the people living in the modern world would agree that dipping is pretty disgusting. If the health hazards are not enough to sway you toward quitting, think of how your addiction makes you look. The smell of tobacco is not the most pleasant, whether you admit it or not. And, in case you have gotten used to it, believe me when I say that other people around you definitely notice it. Tobacco stains also don't look very attractive all over your teeth, no matter what your mom and your girlfriend might tell you.

Chapter 2: Know Your Addiction

If you are reading this book, you probably already understand you have an addiction. The good thing is that I'm not here to judge you or ridicule you it, but instead, I'm here to help you get rid of it. If you're still not sure whether or not you have an addiction, just look back at how long you have been using tobacco and that will answer your question. Remember how I explained earlier that dipping is not a safe alternative to smoking, because it actually contains a greater amount of nicotine than cigarettes? Well, another way to think of it is that thirty minutes of dipping has the same level of nicotine as smoking three cigarettes. If you go through 2 cans a week, you are getting the same amount of nicotine as someone who smokes a pack and a half a day.

Remember, smokeless tobacco is still tobacco and, thus, still contains nitrosamines, which are cancer-causing chemicals from the curing cycle of the product. Regardless of the claim that chewing tobacco improves athletic performance, which is why the professional baseball players do it, let me just clear that up for you here and now: That's simply not true. On the contrary actually, it has been shown that dipping causes an increase in heart rate – something that any athlete doesn't need any extra of, since they're already in the midst of trying to lower their heart rate despite the accelerated physical activity. Not to mention that this increased heart rate can actually cause dangerous heart problems later on in life.

Another common myth from people who are addicted, is that they say even though chewing tobacco destroys the gums, this can be remedied with proper gum care. This is an oxymoron, in a sense, because if you really are taking good care of your gums, chewing tobacco would be the first thing you would avoid. Remember that, once the gums pull away from our teeth, they do not grow back, and brushing your teeth or flossing has proven ineffective when it comes to counteracting or reversing the effects of dipping on the gums and teeth.

Yet probably the biggest myth about dipping is that you can quit anytime. Since dipping tobacco contains around three times the level of nicotine to be released, it is actually a whole lot more addictive than smoking.

If you've been telling yourself any of these little fibs about dipping, trying to make yourself believe it's an acceptable habit, then now's the time to stop. Fess up to yourself: Dipping is not a safer alternative than smoking. Dipping does not enhance athletic performance. Dipping only does damage to your teeth and gums. And, Dipping is very difficult to quit without a determined effort.

Chapter 3: How to Quit Using the PILT Method

Decide to Quit

The decision needs to be made by you. Intervention or peer pressure will not get you over the top when it comes to nicotine addiction. The best way to quit is to decide for yourself that you want to quit. Sure, there can be outside factors, like wanting to live longer for your family, but the actual decision will have to come from you. Focus on all the bad things that dipping gives you – and there are a lot – and compare that to the advantages that you get from the habit, if any. Having a "pros and cons" type of list can really help you at this point. Here are some of the reasons that others have used to kick the habit. Who knows, you might find them helpful too:

> ➤ Improve health and avoid cancers later in life.

> ➤ To get my family and friends back into my life

> ➤ To be a good example to my kids.

➢ To save money that can be used for more productive things, like a vacation I always wanted.

➢ Improve oral hygiene.

➢ To avoid becoming more and more addicted.

➢ It is not socially a good idea anymore.

➢ It's no longer fun, and the taste does not make it easier.

➢ I want to prove to myself that I can do it.

Next, use the PILT method to quit

The PILT method is a 4-step, very straightforward, process to quit dipping. Let's go through the steps now:

Step 1: Pinpoint a Date

A journey of a thousand miles starts with a single step, as they say, and this applies to quitting any addictive behavior or substance. It is not going to be done overnight and you need to have a good plan, and enough discipline to actually follow through with your plan. It is going to be a step-by-step process and, if you look at it that way, you might be amazed at how easy it will be. First, you'll need to pick a date that you're going to quit. You could choose today, but as you'll see in the following few step, you need to do a little planning first. So instead, give yourself about a week to prepare. That way, when the date comes, you will be emotionally and mentally ready.

Meanwhile, try to taper down during this week, just to make your life a lot easier the following week. Do not try to flat out quit in a day, because that can cause massive withdrawals and inevitably lead you to relapse. While some have been successful this way, most people find it a lot easier if you taper down slowly, leading to your actual quit date. That way, you have given your body enough preparation to cope with the changes that you are making. Try not only using smaller amounts, but slowly increase the time period between dips. You may want to go cold turkey and all-out quit in one day, but if you have been addicted to it for a while, tapering down on both amount and time will be your best bet. This will help keep the addiction at bay longer and longer, until you get to your quit date and notice that you no longer have any urge to reach for that tin. This is also the reason why you need to set a quit date that is at least a week away.

Step 2: Identify Obstacles and Plan for Them

Next, you need to look into your crystal ball and think of all the withdrawal symptoms and cravings you might experience when you try to quit. Also, think about all the things that might just go wrong in your life (i.e., your car breaks down on the way to work), that might cause stress resulting in an amplified craving to quit. Make a list of everything you can think of, and then identify "rewards" or "alternatives" to dipping as for how you'll deal with these stressors. For example, you can replace general cravings with gummy bears. Part of planning ahead though, is going to the grocery store and buying a few bags of gummy bears. Sure, that's not the best example because gummy bears aren't too good for you either, but you get the idea.

Step 3: Let Your Friends and Family Know

You have a group of people who love you, and who are your allies. If you let them in on what you're up to, then they can be there to help you through it and support you. If you have a buddy who also dips, ask him not to do it in front of you. If you have a significant other, most likely they'll be thrilled at the news, and may even offer to incentivize your effort somehow, by giving you rewards at certain milestones for staying on track. If you've been heavily addicted for some time, you may even want to chat with your doctor about your quitting, and get his support as well. He may suggest medical aids to help you quit if you need them, such as nicotine patches or nicotine chewing gum. He may also be able to give you good advice about managing the withdrawal symptoms.

Step 4: Throw Out Your Dip

That's right, ALL OF IT! Don't keep a "back-up" can. Just get rid of it all, and don't buy any more. You're a non-dipper now, so you don't need any reminders or easy avenues to give in to a craving.

Now Quit!!!!!!

Now you're ready! Make your quit date a special day from the get-go. After all, you are doing yourself a favor and turning your life around for the better. Start the day with something like a walk or a swim to both relax and boost your energy for the day ahead. Better yet, visit your dentist and have your teeth whitened!

Chapter 4: Coping with Withdrawal

The first couple of weeks after your quit date are going to be quite a challenge; this is where most people relapse. For some, even though they tapered down to this point, they still have some withdrawal symptoms, although these will not last long. You are getting over an addiction and this is to be expected. This is the period when your discipline and devotion to your cause will be truly tested. Some of the withdrawal symptoms of the first week may include:

> **Cravings to Dip.** You will definitely have the urge, especially if you go cold turkey. The best way to approach this problem is to wait it out. Keep yourself busy and take deep breaths; working out helps a lot, since it releases endorphins that counteract the urge.

> **Anxiety and Irritability.** You may feel upset and get ticked off quickly by the smallest things. Walk away from anything that makes you upset and take a few deep breaths. Asking your friends and family to be extra patient with you is also helpful.

➤ **Insomnia or Restlessness.** You may have trouble sleeping at first. But don't worry, this will get better after a few days or a week. Just curl up with a good book, or find productive ways to use your new waking hours so that your mind doesn't go to your craving to dip.

➤ **Constipation.** This is common but, luckily, it can be easily remedied by increasing your fiber intake. Start munching on whole grain bread, fruits, and vegetables.

➤ **Sugar Cravings.** Since you used to get ample sugar from tobacco, your body has become accustomed to having high levels of sweets. The best way to counter this is by reaching for low calorie foods with natural sugars, like apples.

➤ **Mental Blah.** You may experience the occasional mental dullness, where you seem to have brain farts more often than usual. Again, don't worry – this will eventually go away and you'll obtain greater mental clarity as time goes on.

➢ **Weight Gain.** Nicotine does speed up metabolism, so when you quit, you may experience a slight increase in your weight. Have a more balanced diet and get into a fitness program, not only to offset the weight gain, but to address other symptoms of withdrawal.

The second week is going to be a bit easier, once you have addressed the biggest reasons for people to relapse. So, if you can go for a week without tobacco, then you can definitely go for a week more. All you need to do is exert the same discipline and willpower that you used in the first week to get you through this second one. It's likely that the cravings to continue, but distinctly less than they were the week before. There will still be a few times where the thought of reaching for a dip will cross your mind, but resisting will be relatively easy at this point. Try to avoid alcoholic beverages, as alcohol can offset all your efforts to quit. Also, try to avoid places and events that put you in contact with tobacco and may trigger a relapse. This is the same reason you would not leave a six-pack in the fridge of a recovering alcoholic.

Chapter 5: After Week Two – Going the Distance

Congratulations! At this point, you are well on your way to turning your back on an addiction that not only causes you problems today, but would most certainly put you six feet under faster than normal. At this juncture, you will have gone through the whole decision making process, planning and execution of your wish to live a tobacco-free life. You should have gone through two solid weeks of not dipping, which is a great leap toward never chewing that disgusting stuff ever again. Keep using the same motivation that you have used to get to this point. If it was strong enough to keep you off the stuff for two solid weeks, it certainly is strong enough to keep you going. The motivation part is not always the same, but it can have the power to turn things around. However, you still need to make sure that you guard against a relapse.

But what if you do relapse?

The idea is to never slip, but not everybody is perfect. In case you do slip and have a dip, you need to get yourself back on track. Don't look at yourself as a failure just because you took one dip. This is where most feel guilty and simply give up and go back to the habit altogether. Instead of doing that, try to figure out what stressor caused the relapse, and then identify how to make sure it doesn't get the best of you again. You don't need to start all over. Just pick up where you left off, and don't blame yourself. But if you find yourself reaching for a dip, and it's increasing in frequency, you will need to re-evaluate your habits and start over with the PILT method – the whole nine yards. Don't give up, though. Giving up is the worst thing you can do at this point. Talk to your physician for additional help if necessary in the form of medical aids, but never give up altogether. You've already endured so much at this point. You already put forth the effort; make sure that it was not wasted. Look back to the very reason you wanted to quit in the first place.

And if you never relapse, then kudos to you! You have made it through the worst part and are well on your way to having a better life. Yes, a better life, because quitting tobacco not only improves your health, but your social and financial life as well. You have more money to use for other things that you might have been putting on hold for a long time, like a cross-country road trip, leasing a new car, or purchasing that laptop you've had your eye on. You will also notice that people may approach you and talk to you more often now because they do not have to endure that overpowering scent of tobacco on your breath. Hey, while you're at it, you might finally get a date from that gal in your office building that you always wanted to ask out, but always avoided talking to you before. Quitting tobacco will opened a countless number of new doors for you, and will give you more years of life to enjoy walking through them. So be sure to keep going in your journey to quit tobacco for good.

Conclusion

With all the health benefits of quitting the habit, you probably are wondering why you didn't quit a long time ago. Well, that was because you were hooked on the stuff and, though it may not be as worrisome as getting addicted to dangerous drugs such as crack, cocaine, or heroine, smokeless tobacco does still has a strong impact on many aspects of your life. With cancer as one of the biggest health issues in the United States, and indeed the whole world, tobacco is slowly becoming one of the few "legal" substances that is documented to cause millions of deaths every year. However, just because it's legal, does not mean you should keep using it, right? You have lived on both sides of the fence and a life free from tobacco is clearly a better place to be. While you deserve a pat on the back for making the decision to change, it is a never-ending process. Just like an alcoholic, the biggest test is whether you can resist the urge to relapse, even with the temptation just a few feet away. If you can go on despite that, then you are a changed person for the better.

Quitting an addiction is never easy, especially one that has had years to take its firm grip on you. But there's no such thing as too far gone when it comes to any addiction. It is simply a question of willpower and what, or who, you are doing it for. You will not be able to endure much if you have nothing to aim for, but if you have that inspiration and will to change, tobacco is not that hard to quit. It only takes the proper approach and planning, and with luck, a good support system, for you to be well on your way. Nothing worth doing can be done overnight, but once you are able to achieve your goal, it is the best feeling. Is it easy? Not exactly. But is it worth it? Most definitely!

Finally, I'd like to thank you for purchasing this book! If you found it helpful, I'd greatly appreciate it if you'd take a moment to leave a review on Amazon. Thank you!